THE OFFICIAL
WEST BROMWICH
ALBION
FOOTBALL CLUB

ANNUAL 2019

C000193137

WEST BROMWICH
ALBION

Written by Dave Bowler

Designed by Paul Galbraith and John Anderson

A Grange Publication

© 2018. Published by Grange Communications Ltd., Edinburgh, under licence from West Bromwich Albion Football Club. Printed in the EU.

Photographs © West Bromwich Albion Football Club, Laurie Rampling and AMA Photography.

ISBN: 978-1-912595-21-1

WEST BROMWICH AL

me down to lie, In pastures green; He leadeth me, The quiet waters by......

4

CONTENTS

WE WANT
MOORE

Darren Moore took the reins as Albion's caretaker head coach at the end of the 2017/18 season and within a few weeks, he'd become the Premier League's Manager of the Month - not a bad start!

I n those six games, he won away at Manchester United and Newcastle, beat Tottenham at The Hawthorns and got draws against Liverpool (coming back from 2-0 down) and Swansea City. While doing that, he rekindled Albion fans' enthusiasm and excitement and so made himself the first choice to take over as Head Coach.

He was duly appointed in the summer and said, "We need resilience, focus, dedication, hard work. Being back in the Championship it's going to be a tough campaign. There's so many more games, more than we have been used to, but we should be looking forward to it.

"I don't have to say too much to them. They know how important they are and they will play a huge part as our 12th man. I'm pleased to be able to send them this message - get behind us as you always have. Your support is invaluable and we need to do this together."

"WE NEED RESILIENCE, FOCUS, DEDICATION, HARD WORK."

"We'll need that togetherness I have spoken about; everybody has got a part to play and of course that includes the fans.

THE MAGNIFICENT SEVEN!

August 18th 2018 was a red letter day for the Albion as we served up a magnificent seven goals against QPR in our best home league win since May 2007 when we beat Barnsley 7-0.

There was a touch of magic in the air as we beat Rangers 7-1 – before the game, even the programme cover had prophesied that we were going to score that many…

SEVEN again…MAGNIFICENT again!

Hunted by defenders…
Hated by opponents!

James Morrison in "Return of the Seven"

PLAYER PROFILES

SAM JOHNSTONE

Born: 25 March 1993
Position: Goalkeeper
Height: 1.79m
Other Clubs: Manchester United, Oldham, Scunthorpe, Walsall, Yeovil, Aston Villa
Albion Games: 0
Albion Goals: 0

BOAZ MYHILL

Born: 9 November 1982
Position: Goalkeeper
Height: 1.91m
Other Clubs: Aston Villa, Stoke City, Bristol City, Bradford City, Macclesfield, Stockport, Hull City, Birmingham City
Albion Games: 81+1
Albion Goals: 0

JONATHAN BOND

Born: 19 May 1993
Position: Goalkeeper
Height: 1.96m
Other Clubs: Watford, Forest Green, Dagenham & Redbridge, Bury, Reading, Gillingham, Peterborough
Albion Games: 0
Albion Goals: 0

PLAYER PROFILES

AHMED HEGAZI

Born: 25 January 1991
Position: Centre-half
Height: 1.95m
Other Clubs: Ismaily, Fiorentina, Al Ahly
Albion Games: 41+1
Albion Goals: 2

KIERAN GIBBS

Born: 26 September 1989
Position: Left-back
Height: 1.79m
Other Clubs: Arsenal, Norwich
Albion Games: 34+1
Albion Goals: 0

CONOR TOWNSEND

Born: 4 March 1993
Position: Left-back
Height: 1.68m
Other Clubs: Hull, Grimsby, Chesterfield, Carlisle, Dundee United, Scunthorpe
Albion Games: 0
Albion Goals: 0

PLAYER PROFILES

KYLE BARTLEY

Born: 22 May 1991
Position: Centre-half
Height: 1.85m
Other Clubs: Arsenal, Sheffield United, Rangers, Swansea, Birmingham City, Leeds
Albion Games: 0
Albion Goals: 0

TOSIN ADARABIOYO

Born: 26 September 1997
Position: Centre-half
Height: 1.96m
Other Clubs: Manchester City
Albion Games: 0
Albion Goals: 0

CRAIG DAWSON

Born: 6 May 1990
Position: Central defender / right-back
Height: 1.88m
Other Clubs: Rochdale
Albion Games: 171+9
Albion Goals: 13

PLAYER PROFILES

KYLE EDWARDS

Born: 17 February 1998
Position: Striker
Height: 1.72m
Other Clubs: Exeter City
Albion Games: 0
Albion Goals: 0

GARETH BARRY

Born: 23 February 1981
Position: Midfielder
Height: 1.83m
Other Clubs: Aston Villa, Manchester City, Everton
Albion Games: 26+3
Albion Goals: 1

CHRIS BRUNT

Born: 14 December 1984
Position: Winger / left-back / midfielder
Height: 1.87m
Other Clubs: Sheffield Wednesday
Albion Games: 323+51
Albion Goals: 45

PLAYER PROFILES

JAMES MORRISON

Born: 25 May 1986
Position: Central midfielder
Height: 1.80m
Other Clubs: Middlesbrough
Albion Games: 250+67
Albion Goals: 39

JAKE LIVERMORE

Born: 14 November 1989
Position: Midfielder
Height: 1.80m
Other Clubs: Tottenham Hotspur, Hull City
Albion Games: 46+7
Albion Goals: 2

REKEEM HARPER

Born: 8 March 2000
Position: Midfielder
Height: 1.88m
Other Clubs: Blackburn Rovers
Albion Games: 0+2
Albion Goals: 0

PLAYER PROFILES

JONATHAN LEKO

Born: 24 April 1999
Position: Winger
Height: 1.82m
Other Clubs: Bristol City
Albion Games: 3+13
Albion Goals: 0

HARVEY BARNES

Born: 9 December 1997
Position: Midfielder
Height: 1.74m
Other Clubs: Leicester City, MK Dons, Barnsley
Albion Games: 0
Albion Goals: 0

MATT PHILLIPS

Born: 13 March 1991
Position: Winger
Height: 1.85m
Other Clubs: Wycombe, Blackpool, QPR
Albion Games: 53+10
Albion Goals: 8

PLAYER PROFILES

SAM FIELD

Born: 8 May 1998
Position: Midfielder
Height: 1.86m
Other Clubs: None
Albion Games: 12+10
Albion Goals: 1

TYRONE MEARS

Born: 18 February 1983
Position: Defender
Height: 1.75m
Other Clubs: Manchester City, Preston North End, West Ham United, Derby County, Marseille, Burnley, Bolton Wanderers, Seattle, Atlanta, Minnesota
Albion Games: 0
Albion Goals: 0

OLIVER BURKE

Born: 7 April 1997
Position: Winger
Height: 1.88m
Other Clubs: Nottingham Forest, RB Leipzig
Albion Games: 2+14
Albion Goals: 0

PLAYER PROFILES

HAL ROBSON-KANU

Born: 21 May 1989
Position: Striker
Height: 1.85m
Other Clubs: Reading
Albion Games: 15+39
Albion Goals: 5

JAY RODRIGUEZ

Born: 29 July 1989
Position: Striker
Height: 1.85m
Other Clubs: Burnley, Southampton
Albion Games: 36+6
Albion Goals: 11

DWIGHT GAYLE

Born: 17 October 1990
Position: Striker
Height: 1.74m
Other Clubs: Dagenham & Redbridge, Bishop's Stortford, Peterborough, Crystal Palace, Newcastle
Albion Games: 0
Albion Goals: 0

WORLD CUP

A TEAM OF ALBION MEN WHO'VE APPEARED AT THE GREATEST SHOW ON EARTH.

BEN FOSTER

England were already out of the 2014 World Cup by the time Roy Hodgson turned to Ben Foster for the third and final group match, a dead rubber against Costa Rica. As you'd expect, Ben stepped up to the mark and kept a clean sheet as England finally got a point on the board in a 0-0 draw against the eventual group winners.

DON HOWE

As we'll see, the 1958 World Cup was an Albion jamboree and Don Howe played his full part in it, featuring in all four of England's games, part of an unbroken run of 23 caps that made up his entire international career. With his attacking style, getting forward and sometimes going beyond the winger, Howe was ahead of his time at right-back.

DIEGO LUGANO

Technically still an Albion man at the 2014 World Cup, though he was soon to move on, the Uruguayan centre-half skippered his side in their opening group game of the competition, a 3-1 defeat to Costa Rica. He then missed the rest of the tournament with injury as his side went out in the last 16.

GONZALO JARA

Jara has made it to two World Cups with Chile but it was at the 2010 tournament that he carried the torch for the Albion. He was a substitute in their opening win over Honduras, keeping his place as they beat the Swiss before losing to Spain. They had the misfortune to meet Brazil in the round of 16, losing 3-0, Jara continuing at centre-back.

STUART WILLIAMS

Stuart was another of the Albion cohort at the 1958 World Cup and, perhaps surprisingly, he was the most successful of the lot as he played a full part in helping Wales come through their group, putting out Hungary on the way, to then meet Brazil in the quarter-finals. Despite missing John Charles, Wales pushed them all the way, the game's only goal scored by a 17-year-old World Cup debutant called Pelé.

THROSTLES

BOBBY ROBSON

Robson was an integral part of the 1958 England squad. Though he's in the middle for us, as he would have been but for injury in 1962, he was an inside-forward at this tournament, having a goal disallowed in the group stages that, had it stood, would have seen England through. Instead they were defeated by the USSR in a play-off for which Robson was controversially dropped.

JUNICHI INAMOTO

Inamoto was our representative at the 2006 World Cup in Germany. It was a disappointing tournament for Japan as they finished bottom of a tough group that also included Brazil, Australia and Croatia. Missing the opening defeat against Australia, Ina came on at half-time in the 0-0 draw with Croatia and started the 4-1 defeat to Brazil.

WILLIE JOHNSTON

So magnificent was Willie's form in 1977/78 that he kept Laurie Cunningham out of our side as he booked his place in Scotland's ill-fated trip to Argentina. With Ally MacLeod promising to win the World Cup, the Scots lost their opener 3-1 to Peru. Johnston failed a drugs test he wasn't supposed to take - deputising for Archie Gemmill - because of an over-the-counter medicine and was sent home. Still an indisputable Albion God.

DEREK KEVAN

The Tank scored eight goals in 14 England games but was never flavour of the month with the press, who criticised his old-fashioned virtues of power and directness. But Kevan scored two of England's four at the 1958 World Cup and had he had better service - Tom Finney was injured in the first game and then winger Bobby Charlton dropped for the play-off - England might have survived the group stage.

JEFF ASTLE

The King's inclusion in the 1970 World Cup squad was touch-and-go but devastating form in the warm-ups sealed his selection. He got his chance as a substitute in the searing midday Mexican sun against Brazil, Emlyn Hughes later saying the subs were all falling asleep in the heat. A chance came his way almost immediately, Astle firing wide of the Brazilian goal, an inconsequential miss in the bigger picture but one magnified by the media.

CHRIS WOOD

At just 18, Chris formed part of the New Zealand squad to reach the World Cup in 2010. It was an uninviting group that included holders Italy, Slovakia and Paraguay. Wood came on as a sub in all three games as the Kiwis went home unbeaten after three draws, Wood having the great Cannavaro on toast at one point.

2017/18 SEASON REVIEW

IT STARTED WELL, IT ENDED WELL, BUT THE BITS IN THE MIDDLE? NOT SO GOOD!

It was a strange season for the Throstles, one that had promised so much and yet ended in huge disappointment as we dropped out of the Premier League after eight consecutive seasons at the top.

Not that we haven't suffered relegations before. For a club of our size, retaining a top-flight place is never easy, even in the years before the Premier League arrived and helped the big six get even bigger. We've had to take the drop plenty of times in the past and we always come back sooner or later, so let's not be too downhearted!

After all, there were plenty of reasons for optimism in the last six games of the season once Darren Moore took charge of the side and began to turn things around, not only ending a nine-game losing streak but going unbeaten in five games and winning the Manager of the Month award for April to boot.

It was all very different back in August when we reeled off wins at home to Bournemouth and away at Burnley and were 13 minutes away from making it three out of three at home to Stoke, eventually drawing that one.

But from there, despite bringing in new players in the transfer window like Grzegorz Krychowiak, Kieran Gibbs and Oliver Burke, things started to fall away from us. It started with a bad day at Brighton and was made worse by some decisions that went against us at Arsenal and then late equalisers conceded to Watford and Leicester.

By the time we lost to Chelsea in October, it seemed we needed a change and out went Tony Pulis after nearly three years at the club, Gary Megson briefly taking charge as Albion drew with Tottenham at Wembley and then picked up another point at home to Newcastle United, Academy graduate Sam Field nabbing his first goal for the club.

Alan Pardew was then announced as Albion's new head coach and endured a tricky start to his new job as we had to face the likes of Liverpool, Manchester United, Arsenal and Everton in his first month. Encouragingly, only United could beat us and when Pardew secured his first

Premier League win as we beat Brighton 2-0, it looked as if things were on the up for the Albion.

That was especially true when we drew at Everton and then won 3-2 in the FA Cup at Anfield on a crazy night when VAR took on WBA – and lost!

That set us up for a crucial run of games against the likes of Southampton, Huddersfield, Watford, Leicester, Bournemouth and Burnley, games that would give us a great chance to climb the table and seek safety.

Unfortunately we lost every one of those games as part of a nine-game losing run that also saw us out of the FA Cup and then saw Alan Pardew out of the Albion, Darren Moore called in to hold the fort as caretaker boss to the end of the season.

Darren immediately stopped the rot as the Throstles held the Swans to a 1-1 draw at The Hawthorns and then it started to get really interesting! With Albion supposedly already doomed to the drop, we won at Manchester United thanks to a Jay Rodriguez goal.

Then we came back from 2-0 down to draw 2-2 with Liverpool thanks to two late goals.

Next we went to Newcastle and won. And we even survived game 37, defeating Tottenham 1-0 in injury time thanks to Jake Livermore's goal as The Hawthorns went ballistic!

The dream ended elsewhere when Southampton beat Swansea to send us down, but at least we went down with dignity, with our heads held high and with some real optimism ahead of the Championship campaign!

STATS

DATE	OPPONENTS	SCORE	GOALS
Saturday 12 August	AFC Bournemouth	1-0	Hegazi
Saturday 19 August	Burnley	1-0	Robson-Kanu
Tuesday 22 August	Accrington Stanley (EFL 2)	3-1	Phillips, Rondon, Rodriguez
Sunday 27 August	Stoke City	1-1	Rodriguez
Saturday 9 September	Brighton	1-3	Morrison
Saturday 16 September	West Ham United	0-0	
Wednesday 20 September	Manchester City (EFL3)	1-2	Yacob
Monday 25 September	Arsenal (ko 8pm)	0-2	
Saturday 30 September	Watford	2-2	Evans, Rondon
Monday 16 October	Leicester City	1-1	Chadli
Saturday 21 October	Southampton	0-1	
Saturday 28 October	Manchester City	2-3	Rodriguez, Phillips
Saturday 4 November	Huddersfield Town	0-1	
Saturday 18 November	Chelsea	0-4	
Saturday 25 November	Tottenham Hotspur	1-1	Rondon
Tuesday 28 November	Newcastle United	2-2	Robson-Kanu, Field
Saturday 2 December	Crystal Palace	0-0	
Saturday 9 December	Swansea City	0-1	
Wednesday 13 December	Liverpool	0-0	
Sunday 17 December	Manchester United	1-2	Barry
Saturday 23 December	Stoke City	1-3	Rondon
Tuesday 26 December	Everton	0-0	
Saturday 31 December	Arsenal	1-1	Rodriguez
Tuesday 2 January	West Ham United	1-2	McClean
Saturday 6 January	Exeter City (FA Cup 3)	2-0	Rondon, Rodriguez
Saturday 13 January	Brighton	2-0	Dawson, Evans
Saturday 20 January	Everton	1-1	Rodriguez
Saturday 27 January	Liverpool (FA Cup 4)	3-2	Rodriguez 2, Matip (og)
Wednesday 31 January	Manchester City	0-3	
Saturday 3 February	Southampton	2-3	Hegazi, Rondon
Monday 12 February	Chelsea	0-3	
Saturday 17 February	Southampton (FA Cup 5)	1-2	Rondon
Saturday 24 February	Huddersfield Town	1-2	Dawson
Saturday 3 March	Watford	0-1	
Saturday 10 March	Leicester City	1-4	Rondon
Saturday 17 March	AFC Bournemouth	1-2	Rodriguez
Saturday 31 March	Burnley	1-2	Rondon
Saturday 7 April	Swansea City	1-1	Rodriguez
Sunday 15 April	Manchester United	1-0	Rodriguez
Sunday 22 April	Liverpool	2-2	Rondon, Livermore
Saturday 28 April	Newcastle United	1-0	Phillips
Saturday 5 May	Tottenham Hotspur	1-0	Livermore
Sunday 13 May	Crystal Palace	0-2	

BARNES STORMER!

Harvey Barnes, Albion's loan signing from Leicester City, wasted no time in making himself a firm favourite with the fans, scoring on his senior debut for the club, an absolute screamer against Bolton Wanderers at The Hawthorns.

And that might be just the start for a player determined to light up Albion's season this term.

"I'm a positive player. I love scoring and making goals. I try to be as creative as I can be on the pitch. But first things first, I want to be part of the team and have a successful season. I want the same as everyone at the club - hoping for promotion.

"On a personal level it would be hitting my targets for goals and assists. And playing in a lot of games. Game time is very important to me.

"I've enjoyed my last two loans at MK Dons and Barnsley - the whole process of it, meeting new players and settling into a team.

"I'M A POSITIVE PLAYER. I LOVE SCORING AND MAKING GOALS."

"The excitement of going out every Saturday in front of a crowd is the main thing I enjoy. You go into some games with 25,000 people in the Championship. Every week is a different test and there's some big clubs.

"I got speaking to Leicester about what was going to happen this season. They said they were happy for me to go out on loan again. I heard about the West Brom interest, took a liking to the club and thought it was probably the right place for me to go.

"They have great ambition for this season. I spoke to the gaffer. The way he's put the club across and the way he wants to play will suit my game."

SAM'S THE MAN

There was a changing of the guard between the goalposts at the end of the 2017/18 season with long-term stalwart Ben Foster moving on. Coming in to replace him came 25-year-old Sam Johnstone, joining us from Manchester United on a four-year deal.

Sam previously enjoyed a strong season on loan with Aston Villa which fell just short of promotion in the Wembley Play-Off Final.

On joining the Throstles, Sam made it clear he is relishing the chance to "settle down" at a club and move his game "up to the next level."

"I'm happy to be here", he said. "I've spoken to a lot of people about the club and heard nothing but good things.

"It's good to get through the door. I've played Championship games and won a promotion from League One with Preston, but always seemed to end back at Manchester United then going somewhere else.

"NOW IT'S TIME TO SETTLE DOWN AND TAKE MY GAME UP TO THE NEXT LEVEL WHICH I BELIEVE I CAN DO HERE."

Head Coach Darren Moore was delighted to get the first signing of his regime into the squad - a signing he believes represents everything he will be trying to build in the months ahead.

"Sam is young and determined to be the best keeper he can possibly be - he's hungry to do that with us at Albion," said Darren.

"We've had him targeted from the outset and we're all delighted to have him on board. He buys into exactly what we are trying to achieve."

23

YOU ARE THE REF

1 EXTRA BALL
It is the last minute of injury time at the end of a match, the ball is in the crowd and they refuse to hand it back for the throw in to the opposition. The taker grabs the spare ball from the ball boy, takes the throw in and, just as his team-mate heads it in, the original ball is thrown back into the area. What do you do?

3 ONE-ON-ONE
A striker is through on goal in a one-on-one with the opposing goalkeeper. He is pulled down but as you blow your whistle and signal for a penalty, you see the ball roll on into the net. What actions do you now take?

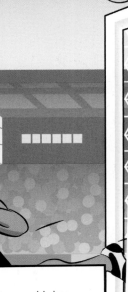

2 SUPER SAVE
A goalkeeper seems to make a world class fingertip save and is congratulated by his defenders - he even pumps the air - but as the opposition try to take a quick corner you are convinced that the keeper never actually touched the ball, your linesman isn't sure so what do you decide ?

5 RUGBY TACKLE
A long ball forward totally bamboozles the opposing goal-keeper and the ball bounces over his head as he rushes out to intercept it. A defender and two attackers chase after it and the defender rugby tackles the striker in front to the ground. The other attacker is clear though and taps the ball into the net. What is your decision?

4 EMBARRASSING MOMENT
The score stands at 2-2 in the dying seconds of a match and, as a shot comes flying towards your face, well off-target of the goal, you instinctively put your hands up to shield yourself. You are then horrified as the ball flies into the net. What now?

6 PENALTY SHOOTOUT
It's a cup game and you are into extra time. The home team's star striker gets injured and can't continue. All the substitutes have been used so the home side has to play on with only ten men. They make it to the penalty shoot-out and the same star striker wants to take a penalty as he now says he is fit again as the injury has passed. Do you let him?

ANSWERS

1. EXTRA BALL
Answer: If the original ball that is thrown back into the penalty box hasn't interfered with play in your opinion then you award the goal! If, however, the ball has interfered with play, you must disallow the goal. You need to be sure!

2. SUPER SAVE
Answer: It is your decision, decide quickly and stick to it regardless of what the players and crowd think. If you think the goalkeeper didn't touch it then award the goal kick and not the corner.

3. ONE-ON-ONE
Answer: Firstly, if you have blown the whistle and signalled a penalty then you must stand by that and not award the goal. Ideally, you should have delayed your decision when the incident happened and you could then have allowed the goal by playing the advantage. You should also send off the goalkeeper.

4. EMBARRASSING MOMENT
Answer: You have scored the winner, as embarrassing as that may be. You need to calm everyone down and explain that the officials are part of the field of play as are the bar, goalposts and corner flags. The goal must stand!

5. RUGBY TACKLE
Answer: Award the goal and then show a yellow card to the defender for unsporting behaviour. You cannot give him a red card as the other attacker obviously had a goal-scoring opportunity so, in effect, the defender didn't deny that goal-scoring opportunity. You correctly played the advantage and the goal was scored.

6. PENALTY SHOOT-OUT
Answer: No, you do not. Only the players who finished the match may take penalties but what you do have to do is make the numbers even by instructing the other team to remove one of their penalty takers. If the player in question had come back onto the pitch before the final whistle at the end of extra time, he could have taken a penalty.

COVER UP!

Hopefully, buying a programme is part of your matchday ritual when you come to The Hawthorns - there's all manner of Albion goodies inside!

The way the programme looks has changed a lot over the years since the first Albion News was published in September 1905. Back in those early days, the cover was given over to an advert but by the 1950s we wanted to advertise ourselves, hence the arrival of the "headless man" on the front cover!

He was the first in a series of graphic designs that defined the seasons, including the view from the Smethwick that we used in the mid-1960s. That gave way to a different style and shape as we moved into the '70s before match action started to feature at the end of the decade, a different cover for every game at last!

We got the crayons out in 1992/93, then launched the first ever 100-page match programme for our first-ever Premier League season in 2002/03. Then we got the players more involved, copying famous record covers in 2016/17 – who knew Jonas Olsson would look so good as David Bowie?!?

YOUNG GUNS
GO FOR IT!

Albion's 2018/19 Carabao Cup campaign got off to a sparkling start for our promising Academy stars as a string of new faces pushed their way into the limelight in the early rounds of the competition.

Rekeem Harper made his first senior start, Jonathan Leko and Sam Field featured prominently in the team, Kyle Edwards and Kyle Howkins both made their debuts and young Morgan Rogers even got on the subs' bench the week after getting his GCSE results!

Better yet, both Edwards and Leko got themselves their first ever Albion goals as we beat Mansfield Town in round two, putting their names on the map and into Darren Moore's thoughts for the season ahead.

Albion's Academy is on the march – you heard it here first!

COACH TRIP!

ALBION HAVE A NEW MAN IN CHARGE as we go into the Championship season, so we've put together a crossword featuring some of Darren Moore's predecessors in the role. See how you get on tracking them down!

ACROSS

1. Tony _____ joined us in January 2015 and took us into the top ten. (5)

3. Player/Manager as we won promotion in 1976. (4,5)

5. Had a short-lived stay at the Albion in 2017/18. (4,6)

7. Roy _____ left us to become England boss in 2012. (7)

8. FA Cup-winning boss in 1968. (4,6)

9. Tony _____ won the Championship in 2008. (7)

DOWN

1. ____ Mel came from Spain to take charge in 2014. (4)

2. We played champagne football under this manager in the late 1970s and early '80s. (3,8)

4. Gary _____ twice won promotion with Albion in the 2000s. (6)

6. Steve _____ took Albion to our best Premier League finish in 2013. (6)

Answers on page 61.

DARREN MOORE
MY FAVOURITE THINGS

Favourite goal?

Darren Carter scored a screamer past Jens Lehmann of Arsenal, we won the game 2-1.

Favourite game?

The 1-0 win at Bradford when Igor Bališ scored the penalty in injury time to set us up for promotion.

Favourite Albion memory?

Scoring the first goal against Palace when we got promoted.

Favourite stadium?

Old Trafford

Favourite opponent?

Thierry Henry

Favourite chocolate bar?

Definitely Twix

Favourite holiday destination?

Jamaica

Favourite TV show?

Match of the Day

Favourite car?

Bentley

BOND
LICENCED TO SAVE!

Albion continued to reshape the goalkeeping department after the departure of Ben Foster when Jonathan Bond became another of the club's summer signings.

The 25-year-old goalkeeper, who penned a two year deal at The Hawthorns, is a former England Under-21s team-mate of Sam Johnstone, having spent time together away on Young Lions duty back in 2013.

Bond, previously of Watford, Reading, Peterborough United, Gillingham and Bury, is keen to push the former Manchester United stopper for the No. 1 jersey and expects there to be an enjoyable but focused atmosphere in training.

He said, "Sam and I have always got on well. We've known each other from England U21s and it's always nice to know someone when you're coming into a new club.

"SAM'S A GOOD GOALKEEPER AND I AM HERE TO CHALLENGE AS BEST I CAN. IT'S EXCITING TO WORK WITH THAT KIND OF QUALITY."

"The goalkeepers spend most of the day with each other so that has made it very easy for me to settle. We're going to look forward to working together throughout the season. Neil Cutler heads up the department and there's a good atmosphere, as well as a high standard, within the group.

"Sam's a good goalkeeper and I am here to challenge as best I can. It's exciting to work with that kind of quality. I've had experience of my own in the Championship before. I feel comfortable at this level."

GOAL OF THE SEASON

There was only one real choice for Albion's goal of the season - Salomón Rondón's vicious Venezuelan volley against Southampton in the FA Cup at The Hawthorns.

With Albion having just gone 2-0 down, a quick reply was essential and it came from the No. 9's left boot.

Watching a looping ball forward dip over his shoulder before smiting it into the goal, Rondón's effort was worthy of being mentioned in the same breath as perhaps our greatest FA Cup goal of all, Tony Brown's miracle against Sheffield Wednesday at Hillsborough in 1970, albeit that Bomber hit his from a fair bit further out.

One to remember for the 2017/18 season, and for Rondón!

GAYLE THE GOAL!

Dwight Gayle loves scoring goals, and that's what he's looking to do to aid Albion's promotion mission after joining on a season-long loan from Newcastle United.

"Scoring goals is one of the best feelings. I love scoring goals and hopefully I can score as many as I can here.

"It's a difficult league to get used to. You need a bit of variety. At Newcastle we didn't start strongly when we went down into this league, but it was about mentality, getting results and building on performances each week.

"THE WHOLE CLUB IS MOVING IN THE RIGHT DIRECTION TOWARDS GETTING PROMOTED THIS SEASON."

"I know the experience and quality we have in the dressing room. I'm looking forward to getting out there, performing, making the fans happy and getting promoted.

"I've spoken to the few of the boys who play here and they've all had good things to say. I spoke to James Morrison and I know Jake Livermore from when I was younger.

"The whole club is moving in the right direction towards getting promoted this season. We've got a great team and we're all focused on achieving our aim."

Darren Moore was delighted to get his man, saying, "Dwight is a proven goalscorer in the Championship and to have someone with that goal threat and prowess in our numbers was attractive to us.

"I believe that Dwight's talents will soon establish him as a fans' favourite. He is quick, sharp off the back of the last defender and is a natural goalscorer - left foot, right foot, in all positions. Somebody with those qualities where it really matters is going to be very important to us."

IT'S A GOAL!!!

```
N K L R K D F F C K R P Y
L B H Y G L D C J Z N N S
V T R O B E R T S L E K P
M X K T B J J Z U N L R I
H M B R O W N K O L L N L
T K T T T P A S N H A T L
H A K P L K D S V W E N I
U X Y F U R T W I L B V H
N D W L A H T R T G R Q P
T L O H O T H S H N E J T
C D C B L R A D L R C R R
E I G N I W M E D O V V K
R N X R N E T K L K Y F G
```

We've hidden the names of a dozen great
Albion goalscorers from across the years in
the puzzle above. Can you find them?

ALLEN   ODEMWINGIE
ASTLE   PHILLIPS
BROWN   REGIS
DOBIE   RICHARDSON
HUNT   ROBERTS
LUKAKU   TAYLOR

Answers on page 61.

THE BIG QUIZ

Albion will be spending 2018/19 in the Championship, so we thought we'd test your knowledge of our new opponents – you might need to ask your family for help on a few of them!

06 BRENTFORD
Former Albion youngster Romaine Sawyers was Brentford Player of the Year last season. Where did he join them from?

07 NORWICH CITY
Which double promotion-winning Albion boss started his managerial career at Norwich in 1995?

08 STOKE CITY
Albion's first-ever league game came against Stoke on September 3rd 1888. True or false?

09 MIDDLESBROUGH
Albion once had Britain's most expensive player when we bought a Middlesbrough man for £516,000 in January 1979. Who was he?

10 QPR
Albion clinched the Championship with a 2-0 win at Loftus Road in May 2008. Who scored?

11 SHEFFIELD WEDNESDAY
Albion bought Chris Brunt to The Hawthorns from Wednesday for £3 million, but in what year?

01 BLACKBURN ROVERS
Former Albion boss Tony Mowbray is in charge of Blackburn now, but from which club did he join Albion?

02 WIGAN ATHLETIC
Goalie Tomasz Kuszczak produced the "save of the season" at Wigan in January 2006 - but whose shot did he save?

03 READING
At the end of 2003/04, Albion fans had a fancy dress 'Vikings' day at Reading for our player of the season. Who was he?

04 SHEFFIELD UNITED
The Blades had three men sent off in the 'Battle of Bramall Lane' against Albion in 2002. Simon Tracey was one - who were the other two?

05 DERBY COUNTY
Derby beat Albion 1-0 in the Play-Off final in 2007. Who scored their goal?

12 NOTTINGHAM FOREST
We hadn't been there since 2009/10 before August's game – what's the name of Forest's stadium?

13 BIRMINGHAM CITY
We last played Birmingham in the FA Cup in 2015 and won 2-1 at St. Andrew's. Who got both goals?

14 SWANSEA CITY
Which Albion man scored a hat-trick of headers against Swansea at The Hawthorns in December 2016?

15 MILLWALL
Albion have never played Millwall in a top-flight league game. True or false?

16 IPSWICH TOWN
Albion got Gareth McAuley on a free transfer from Ipswich in the summer of 2011. Who was our manager then?

17 BOLTON WANDERERS
We met Bolton in the 2001 Play-Off semi-final. What was the aggregate score?

18 LEEDS UNITED
Which country has Leeds striker and former Albion man Tyler Roberts represented?

19 BRISTOL CITY
Bristol City nearly put us out of the FA cup in 2016 – who scored our last gasp equaliser at The Hawthorns?

20 PRESTON NORTH END
Albion have played Preston in two separate FA Cup finals. True or false?

21 HULL CITY
The most money Hull have received in selling a player is £11 million for a former Albion man they sold to Southampton in August 2014. Who?

22 ROTHERHAM UNITED
A legendary Albion centre-forward made his debut against Rotherham in the League Cup in 1977, scoring twice in a 4-0 win. Who?

23 ASTON VILLA
Which player who started his league career with Aston Villa, broke the Premier League's appearances record while with Albion?

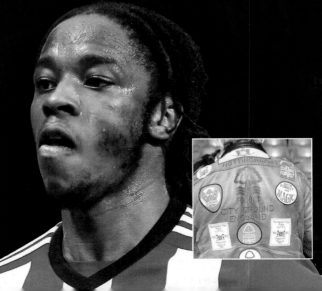

THAT'S TOE-SIN ADA-RAH-BYE-YO!

It may not be easy to pronounce the name of new Albion central defender Tosin Adarabioyo – he even spells it out for people on his Twitter bio! – but it's easy to see Albion have got themselves a terrific player on loan from Manchester City.

Darren Moore was delighted to sign one of the few men in football who can actually look down on him – physically speaking of course…

"Tosin is a young man but in terms of his football age, he is way in advance of his years. We've seen a number of young players prove that they are good enough to make an impression on the world stage and he falls into that bracket," said Darren.

"HE WILL 100% BE A FIRST TEAM CONTENDER."

"I feel this is a fantastic opportunity for him and for the club. He has speed, balance, presence. He's very comfortable in possession of the ball and he will 100% be a first team contender."

For Tosin, coming to terms with new surroundings after a lifetime at City is part of the challenge: "It feels very strange considering the amount of time I've been at Manchester City," he said. I think it's the time in my career where I need to play as many games as I can. The challenge of the Championship is playing two games a week, so it's about adapting to that.

"Darren Moore was a big part of my decision. He's a great guy. I can't wait to start working under him. In terms of his personality, how he comes across and his history of being a centre-half, I think I can learn a lot from him."

'BLIND DAVE' HEELEY

Nobody is a greater example of The Albion Foundation's motto 'Inspire to Achieve', than the charity's ambassador 'Blind Dave' Heeley.

Aged ten, Dave was diagnosed with Retinitis Pigmentosa, an inherited condition of the eye that leads to loss of vision and blindness. Losing his eyesight completely by his early 20s, the man from the Midlands has gone on to raise over £100,000 for Albion's official charity.

The Baggies superfan continues to inspire people in the community and those further afield, as Rob Lake, Albion Foundation Director, explains; *"Once met, he just inspires you completely. He gives you a different perspective on life.*

"The man just has positivity running through his veins and you just become galvanised by him. He is one of the most genuine, inspirational men I have ever met in my life. He's always thinking of others and the way he's taken the Foundation to his heart, he just can't do enough for the charity."

Dave's list of endurance challenges includes the 'Top 2 Toe' challenge where he ran from John O'Groats to Land's End - that's ten marathons in ten days, with hundreds of miles of cycling on top!

He's completed the gruelling Marathon des Sables, an event covering 156 miles over six days and being totally self-sufficient in the boiling heat of the Sahara Desert. The physical feats accomplished means he has travelled more than two laps of the earth by foot, bike or water.

In 2017, the lifelong Albion fan was awarded with the 'Freedom of The Hawthorns' at the Foundation's 25-year anniversary dinner.

Albion's Chris Brunt has great admiration for the endurance star, saying *"He's a great guy and he's an inspiration to everybody. He sums up everything that the Albion Foundation is about."*

With such demanding fundraising challenges completed in the name of the Foundation, Dave explains what makes him put his body through the challenges for the charity:

"The Albion Foundation does some marvellous work in the local community. They are really passionate about helping children and adults with disabilities and learning difficulties, both in playing sport and making the transition from full-time education into work.

"I would like to put the message across to all these kids, everything is possible. Anything is possible. Don't just sit on your laurels, if there's something you want to do within reason, if you want to do it, you make your mind up and you go and do it."

TO CAP IT ALL!

THERE'S NOTHING QUITE LIKE PLAYING FOR THE ALBION

and we're going to make sure that everybody who gets that honour understands just what a privilege it is.

As you all know, when a footballer plays for his country, he is awarded a cap to mark the occasion.

It seemed to us that playing for England, Scotland, Wales and the like, it's all very nice, but it's not like playing for the Albion, is it?!

So last year, we decided that we are going to reward every player – past, present and future - who has represented us in the league with a special Albion cap.

Every player who plays a league game for the Throstles will get an individually tailored cap which contains the number they are in the Albion chain of debutants – from No. 1, Billy Bassett, to No. 911, Daniel Sturridge, and beyond into all the seasons to come.

It features the original club crest designed by club secretary, Tom Smith, back in 1884, along with the famous WBA lettering from the late '70s on the back.

Over the course of the next year (or two) we will be tracking down as many of our former players as we possibly can in order to present them with their caps, while we will also be looking for family members from those players who have passed so that the caps can be placed in the right hands in perpetuity.

The first recipients of the caps were the 1968 FA Cup-winning team, presented with their caps at the 50th anniversary dinner held in May 2018.

David Ashman, the son of Albion's manager that day Alan Ashman, presented the caps to Graham Williams, John Kaye, Doug Fraser, Bobby Hope, Ian Collard and Dennis Clarke while Laraine Astle, June Clark, Jenny Osborne and Ena Talbut collected caps on behalf of their husbands. Graham Lovett's widow Kate will receive his at a later date. Tony Brown, who couldn't make the dinner, received his on film from Chris Brunt.

So, we've made our start and begun to give the men who built this football club a lasting memento of their place in our hearts - a timely reminder that whatever our temporary misfortunes might be, there is no other football club like West Bromwich Albion!

JAKE LIVERMORE

WEST BROMWICH ALBION

OPPORTUNITY KNOCKS FOR CONOR

Albion increased their defensive cover this summer when attacking left-back Conor Townsend joined the club from League One Scunthorpe United.

Darren Moore was delighted to get him and said, "He's been on our radar for quite a while and I'm particularly pleased we've been able to get him in because two other clubs were also trying to sign him.

"And there is more to come from him. He's joined an experienced group of players who will be able to help develop him in the working environment we have here."

Conor, 25, was equally thrilled with the switch after playing at Hull and Scunthorpe along with loan spells at Grimsby, Chesterfield, Carlisle and Dundee United.

"It's a massive chance for me. I've worked hard throughout my career to get to this stage and I'm proud of what I've done so far", he said. "As a young player you always want to play at the highest level but sometimes the route isn't straight there and you have to do it the hard way.

"I've plied my trade in the lower leagues. To get a chance here is massive and I want to take it. I want to kick on now and hopefully get Albion back to the Premier League.

"As soon as I knew the club were interested it was always the place I wanted to go. It was a no-brainer coming here as soon as I spoke to the manager about what he wants to do. I've spoken to a lot of people who've been here and they've nothing but good things to say.

"I'm attack-minded. I like to get up and down the pitch and try and affect the game going forward. I like to get crosses in. I've still got stuff to work on - as anyone has - so hopefully I can keep improving and help the team.

"You're always learning off everyone; players and coaching staff. Darren has a wealth of experience that I can tap into. Hopefully he can help me improve but it's also down to me to put the hard work in. The squad here is unbelievable and to come into that group is a privilege."

CHRIS BRUNT
MILESTONE MAN!

THESE ARE MILESTONE DAYS FOR CHRIS BRUNT, ALBION'S LEFT FOOTED WIZARD.

S ailing past 350 appearances for The Throstles, he had 374 games to his name by the end of 2017/18 and has his sights set on plenty more to come.

He is in the Top 20 of Albion appearance makers now, and is chasing down quite a few of those who are above him in the list as he looks to make it 400 games for the Albion.

He's played more internationals than any other player in the history of the club, winning 54 Northern Ireland caps while he's been at The Hawthorns.

He's on the brink of making it 50 goals in his Albion career too, just five more needed for that milestone and this season, he will be looking to emulate Neil Clement by becoming just the second Albion player to win three promotions with the club.

After 11 years at the Albion already, that £3 million transfer fee from Sheffield Wednesday looks like small change doesn't it?

LOYALTY

WISDOM

SIGNED

AUG
15
2007

DEBUT

SEPT
01
2007

374
ALBION APPEARANCES

323 STARTS
51 SUBSTITUTE APPEARANCES

269
PREMIER LEAGUE GAMES

237 STARTS
32 SUBSTITUTE APPEARANCES

343
LEAGUE GAMES

61 STARTS
13 SUBSTITUTE APPEARANCES

FA CUP GAMES	CHAMPIONSHIP GAMES	LEAGUE CUP GAMES
24	**74**	**7**
18 STARTS	61 STARTS	7 STARTS
6 SUBSTITUTE APPEARANCES	13 SUBSTITUTE APPEARANCES	0 SUBSTITUTE APPEARANCES

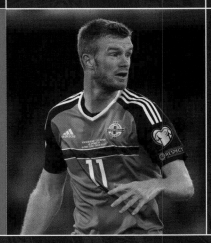

54
INTERNATIONAL CAPS FOR NORTHERN IRELAND
(A CLUB RECORD)

20TH
★ IN THE ★
ALL-TIME ALBION LIST

▼ GOALS

45	24	17	2	2
ALBION GOALS	PREMIER LEAGUE GOALS	CHAMPIONSHIP GOALS	FA CUP GOALS	LEAGUE CUP GOALS

● ● ● 3 GOALS V QPR = MOST AGAINST A SINGLE CLUB

HEADERS	RIGHT FOOT	LEFT FOOT	PENALTIES	FREE-KICKS
6	**3**	**36**	**4**	**7**

15 FROM OUTSIDE THE BOX
30 INSIDE THE BOX
09 INSIDE THE SIX YARD BOX

HARVEY BARNES

WEST BROMWICH ALBION

PUT YOUR LACES THROUGH IT CHRIS!

WHEN ALBION GRABBED A LAST-GASP WINNER AGAINST TOTTENHAM IN THE LAST HOME GAME OF LAST SEASON, ALBION SKIPPER CHRIS BRUNT GOT PRETTY EXCITED ABOUT IT ALL!

Grabbing the ball out of the goal, he then smashed it into the air in celebration – but where exactly did it go?
Can you work it out?!

Answer on page 61.

THE HAWTHORNS THE HOME OF FOOTBALL!

THE THROSTLES HAVE PLAYED AT THE HAWTHORNS FOR MORE THAN 100 YEARS NOW – OUR GROUND WAS THE FIRST NEW FOOTBALL LEAGUE STADIUM OF THE 20TH CENTURY, OPENED ON 3RD SEPTEMBER 1900.

The first game was a 1-1 draw with Derby, their Steve Bloomer scoring the first goal at the ground, Chippy Simmons becoming Albion's first scorer.

Y ou could only get 35,000 people in the ground back in those days but by 1924, capacity had nearly doubled to 65,000 as going to football became more and more popular – you couldn't watch it on TV!

Night games didn't start to happen until the 1950s, Albion installing floodlights in 1957 at a cost of £18,000, the first floodlit game a 1-1 draw with Chelsea on 18th September 1957. The lights were also used for a cricket game in 1980 when a Warwickshire XI played Ian Botham's XI in aid of Alistair Robertson's testimonial!

The Rainbow Stand – which stood where the East Stand now is – was built in 1964 and was called the Rainbow because of its multi-coloured seats. In 1976, in front of the Rainbow, we built our very first executive boxes, a sign of the times.

Halfords Lane was the next to be changed, and between 1979 and 1982, the existing structure was put in place, featuring seats, a press box and directors' box, along with 26 more executive boxes.

After the Hillsborough disaster, the Taylor Report meant we needed to put seats in the Brummie and Smethwick Ends, the stands at either end of the ground completely replaced at a cost of £4.15 million. The first game at the all-seater Hawthorns was against Bristol City on 26th December 1995, Albion winning 1-0.

The Rainbow Stand had outlived its useful life and that whole side of the ground was demolished in 2001 to make way for the £7.5 million East Stand, which is still the main stand at The Hawthorns.

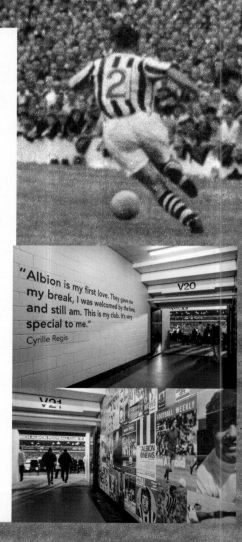

"Albion is my first love. They gave me my break, I was welcomed by the fans, and still am. This is my club. It's very special to me."

Cyrille Regis

The Halfords Lane Stand was extensively modernised in 2008 and is now known as the West Stand, with the directors' box having moved back to that side of the ground.

The Hawthorns is a famous ground not just because of the many great Albion games that have been played there but because it is the highest Football League ground in the country, at 551 feet above sea level.

Albion were also the first club in the country to use the stilecard ticketing system in 2002, also becoming the first club to use big screens in widescreen format at the same time. We updated them in time for the start of the 2017/18 season, bringing in the best screens in the country!

The statue in honour of Tony Brown was another recent addition to things, unveiled in 2014 so that Bomber can watch over us all, day and night.

So next time you come to The Hawthorns remember – you're coming to a historic place!

THE BOYS OF '68

EVERTON *versus* **WEST BROMWICH ALBION**

Saturday 18th May   1968 Kick-off 3pm

Albion's 1968 FA Cup-winning team celebrated the 50th anniversary of their famous day at Wembley in May 2018 as they got together for a special dinner at The Hawthorns. It was all before your time of course, so here's your guide to the guys who won us the cup – just as they were described in the match programme in May 1968!

JOHN OSBORNE, *Goalkeeper*

One of the most reliable goalkeepers in the First Division, Osborne signed for Albion from Chesterfield in January 1967. Tall and agile, Barlborough (Derbyshire) born Osborne was a schoolboy international and played in the same side as Albion pivot John Talbut. This will be his first appearance at Wembley with Albion. He could not play in last year's League Cup Final against Queens Park Rangers because he was cup-tied.
Height: 6ft 2½in. Weight: 12st 4lb.

DOUG FRASER, *Right Back*

Born Eaglesham, near Glasgow, this Scot has been a great asset to the Albion since he signed for them in September 1963. Can play in either wing-half position and also at centre-forward, where he first appeared for his former club Aberdeen. Has been a regular member of the side since making his debut against Birmingham City in September 1963, and made such progress last season that he was picked for the Scottish team on their tour abroad during the close season. Played at Wembley last season against Queens Park Rangers.
Height: 5ft 8¾in. Weight: 11st 4lb.

GRAHAM WILLIAMS, *Left Back (Captain)*

Longest serving player on the staff, joining Albion as a professional in April 1955 after a spell on the groundstaff. Born in Rhyl, he is an experienced Welsh international and has played frequently at Wembley. Made his debut for Albion as an outside-left in November 1955 and also played at wing-half before settling in the left-back berth. First capped by Wales in season 1959/60, he was skipper of the defeated Albion side in last year's League Cup Final.
Height: 5ft 7in. Weight: 12st 3lb.

TONY BROWN, *Righ Half*

Tony Brown is the sort of player most managers would like to have in his team. A great club man who can play ably in numerous positions, notably wing-half, outside-right or inside-forward. Has scored crucial goals for Albion in this year's Cup competition. Born in Oldham, he was discovered by Albion while playing for Manchester Boys and was quickly snapped up as an apprentice. Signed professional in 1963 and played for the England Youth side the same season. Fast, skilful, with a strong shot.
Height: 5ft 6½in. Weight: 11st.

JOHN TALBUT, *Centre Half*

Tall, commanding centre-half who signed for Albion from Burnley in December 1966. This England U-23 international has added much strength to the Albion defence and has been one of the stars of their Cup run this year. Born in Headlington, he went to Burnley from school and quickly made his mark at Turf Moor, with his determined tackling and authority in the air. As a boy, he represented Durham County Schools.
Height: 6ft 1½in. Weight: 13st.

JOHN KAYE, *Left Half*

Signed from Scunthorpe United in May 1963 for a then record fee for the club. Primarily a striker, he has proved a capable midfield player and even played in defence in the second replay against Liverpool. Began career with his native Goole Town side before moving to Scunthorpe in September 1960. This big, bustling forward is a constant danger to defences. A member of the Albion team beaten by QPR in last year's League Cup Final at Wembley.
Height: 5ft 9¾in. Weight: 12st 1lb.

THE FOOTBALL ASSOCIATION CHALLENGE CUP COMPETITION FINAL

GRAHAM LOVETT, *Outside Right*

Birmingham-born, he watched last season's FA Cup Final from his hospital bed where he was still recovering from serious neck injuries sustained in a car crash in December 1966. These injuries threatened to curtail a promising career but such is his strength, both physical and psychological, that he returned to the team this season and will take his place in the Albion team today.

Height: 5ft 10in. Weight: 10st 4lb.

IAN COLLARD, *Inside Right*

A versatile player who has played at inside-forward and full-back as well as in his usual No. 4 jersey. Born Co. Durham, he joined Albion on leaving school and signed professional in November 1964. Another member of the side beaten at Wembley last year, he recently deputised for the injured Bobby Hope with great success.

Height: 5ft 7in. Weight: 11st 7lb.

JEFF ASTLE, *Centre Forward*

Albion's leading League and Cup scorer this season and on the fringe of international honours. He is one of the players most likely to win the trophy for Albion because of his ability to snap up the half chance. Born Eastwood, Notts, he began his career with Notts County in October 1958 before moving to The Hawthorns in September 1964. Tall and commanding, both on the ground and in the air. Can play at either centre-forward or inside-forward. Also a member of the beaten Wembley side last year.

Height: 5ft 11½in. Weight: 11st 3lb.

BOBBY HOPE, *Inside Left*

Missed the first two matches against Liverpool in the sixth round but returned in the second replay and engineered Albion's victory which took them into the semi-final. Joined The Hawthorns groundstaff in July 1959 and made his debut the following year against Arsenal when only 16. A Scottish Schoolboy International, his subtle promptings have been a big reason why Albion are in the Final. Born Bridge of Allan, he played in last year's League Cup Final and toured with the Scottish party last summer.

Height: 5ft 7in. weight: 11st 3lb.

CLIVE CLARK, *Outside-left*

One of the deadliest wingers in the League, his goalscoring ability has made him a target for many First Division clubs. Last year he scored two goals at Wembley for Albion in the League Cup Final against his old club, Queens Park Rangers – and finished on the losing side. This year he hopes to score for the winning side at Wembley. Joined Albion from QPR in January 1961 after previously being on Leeds' books. Born Leeds, he is an England Under-23 international and scored the winning goal against Liverpool in the sixth round.

Height: 5ft 7in. Weight: 10st 2lb.

DENNIS CLARKE, *Substitute*

Born at Stockton-on-Tees and joined Albion from school in 1963. Signed professional in February 1965 and made his league debut the following year against Tottenham Hotspur. Originally a half-back, he was converted to right-back and was such a success that he has now made the position his own. Not very big for a full-back, but a strong tackler and a fine distributor. Was in the Albion side beaten in last year's League Cup Final at Wembley.

Height: 5ft 8¾in. Weight: 11st 7½lb.

ALAN ASHMAN, *Manager*

Mr. Ashman is, at 39, one of a new breed of football managers making their mark. He joined Albion a year ago, agreeing to take up the job on Cup Final day 1967 after leading Carlisle United to promotion from the Third Division and almost right through to the First. As a player, he distinguished himself at centre-forward, scoring 98 goals in 207 games for Carlisle before retiring with a knee injury in 1958.

BARTLEY AT THE BACK

Central defender Kyle Bartley is planning to put his experience of the gruelling Championship campaign to good use after agreeing a three-year deal with the Baggies.

Kyle, who started his career with Arsenal and has been recruited from Swansea City, knows exactly what Albion can expect this season after impressing in Championship loan spells.

His most recent, a stand-out campaign with Leeds United in 2016/17, earned Kyle a four-year deal with Swansea but injuries blighted his progress last season and gave Head Coach Darren Moore the chance to swoop this summer.

"I've got good experience of the Championship; I know what it takes and how long the season is," said Bartley, who also scored five goals in 19 appearances on loan at Birmingham City in the 2013/14 season.

"I'M A NO-NONSENSE CENTRE BACK BUT I LIKE TO PLAY."

"It's hard and it's important to have players who are aware of the ups and downs and are able to maintain a consistent level. I like to think I'm a leader, a committed player who will always give 100 per cent. I play with my heart on my sleeve.

"I'm a no-nonsense centre back but I like to play. I've come from an Academy background (at Arsenal) and with Swansea's style, but I definitely defend first!

"Albion is a massive club and the new manager coming in at the end of last year brought something new and fresh, and after speaking with Darren, I knew this was the place I wanted to be. He let me know his ideas for the season and the next few years, his ambitions for the club and he told me about the fan base and the facilities."

DARREN'S COMING HOME!

Darren Moore might have the right address on the team skip that contains all the players' boots, but can you help him find the way through the maze and back to the dressing room before training starts?

START

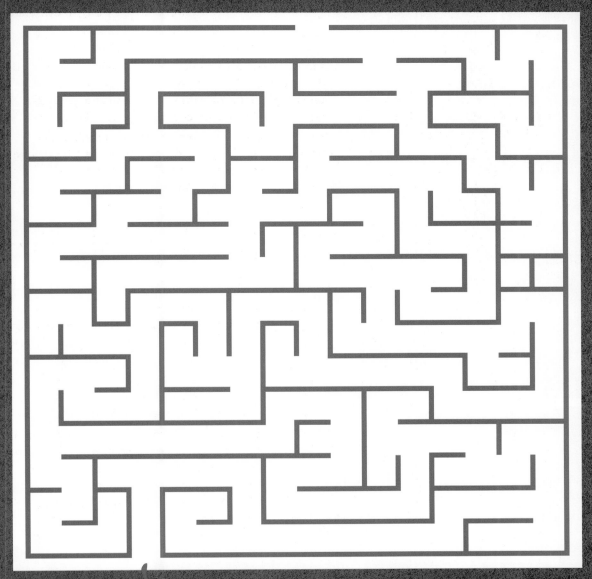

DRESSING ROOM

Answer on page 61.

J-GOAL!

The race to be Albion's top goalscorer of 2017/18 went all the way down to the wire, Salomón Rondón neck and neck with Jay Rodriguez.

But in the end, it was J-Rod who won the photo finish, ending up with 11 goals to the Venezuelan's ten.

There were some crucial strikes from Rodriguez too, popping up with two goals as we humbled Liverpool at Anfield in the FA Cup, becoming the only team to win there all season.

Jay also snatched the winner as we beat Manchester United at Old Trafford as Darren Moore's team pursued a late escape from the drop, but he also got goals at The Hawthorns too!

He was on target against Stoke early in the season, and how about that last-gasp penalty against Arsenal at Christmas to secure the Throstles a draw? Here's hoping for plenty more from Jay in the years to come!

JAZZ UP JOHNSTONE!

Goalkeeper kits tend to be a bit boring don't they? All one colour, nothing to make them stand out?

Here's your chance to change all of that and give Sam a new kit to be proud of. So go ahead, jazz up Johnstone!

THE BEARDED WONDERS

AN ALBION XI TO TERRIFY THE BARBER...

BOAZ MYHILL
Regularly sporting a beard you'd need hedge trimmers to attack properly, Boaz puts some of the others in our hirsute XI to shame. Surprisingly, the ball never got lost in the facial foliage.

CARL HOEFKENS
Following a clean shaven start to life at The Hawthorns, the right-back adopted the "Wolverine" look later on, presumably in an effort to frighten opposition wingers.

JONATHAN GREENING
With more than a passing resemblance to the Shroud of Turin and daft as the proverbial brush, Greening is another underrated recent giant, skipper of the side that won the Championship in 2008.

GABRIEL TAMAS
Gaby had a relatively short Albion stay but one where he made a real impact. Brought in by Roberto Di Matteo in the promotion season, he formed a strong partnership with Jonas Olsson.

PAUL SCHARNER
Devotee of the goatee, the Austrian Scharner was a significant signing by Roberto Di Matteo, crucial in building our self belief. Will always be remembered for the goal that won the game at Villa Park.

LARUS SIGURDSSON
A tackle from Larus was always a terrifying sight for the Icelander gave no quarter, ever. Looked even scarier with a beard.

TONY BROWN
He was at The Hawthorns for so long that he went through pretty much every fashion in "male grooming". The beard stuck around long enough to be immortalised on the promotion winning day at Oldham in 1976.

ROGER MINTON
One of the poor unfortunate youngsters who was ushered into the team a little too early by Don Howe in the 1970s, he had a beard that made him look like a member of Pink Floyd's road crew.

RICKIE LAMBERT
Rickie went for the full on Edward VII / George V set of whiskers during his brief Albion sojourn. Perhaps he joined a season too late, Lambert was a wholehearted trier and a genuinely great pro throughout his stay.

TONY GREALISH
Had a ferocious-looking beard that looked like a pointed weapon ready to stab opponents in the chest, Grealish wanted to win at everything, from tiddlywinks to football.

GARY OWEN
The beard arrived later in his career, perhaps an attempt to add gravitas to the cherubic features that perpetually cast him as an under-21, Owen holding the record number of appearances at that level without going on to claim a full cap.

SAM JOHNSTONE
MY FAVOURITE THINGS

Favourite goal?

Rooney's overhead kick against Man City.

Favourite player?

Growing up, I looked up to Edwin van der Sar.

Favourite school lesson?

P.E!

Favourite animal?

Dog

Favourite drink?

Coke

Favourite holiday?

I never tend to go back to the same one, but I like the Bahamas.

Favourite TV show?

Power

Favourite car?

Ferrari. Haven't got one... yet!

US AND THEM

As Albion embark on a season in the Championship, we're meeting teams we haven't seen in a while. So, to get you fully clued up for 2018/19, here's our league record against the rest of the Championship!

BRISTOL CITY

DERBY COUNTY

ASTON VILLA
P144 / W47 / D32 / L65
Record Win: 7-0 (1935/36)
Record Defeat: 1-7 (1898/99)

ASTON VILLA

BIRMINGHAM CITY
P116 / W49 / D33 / L34
Record Win: 7-1 (1959/60)
Record Defeat: 0-4 (1947/48, 1998/99, 2004/05)

BLACKBURN ROVERS
P112 / W40 / D26 / L46
Record Win: 8-1 (1935/36)
Record Defeat: 2-6 (1888/89)

BOLTON WANDERERS
P134 / W43 / D44 / L47
Record Win: 7-2 (1900/01)
Record Defeat: 0-7 (1889/90)

BRENTFORD
P12 W8 D2 L2
Record Win: 4-3 (1937/38)
Record Defeat: 1-2 (1936/37)

BRISTOL CITY
P40 W16 D12 L12
Record Win: 4-1 (2007/08, 2009/10)
Record Defeat: 1-3 (1905/06, 1977/78)

DERBY COUNTY
P100 W34 D28 L38
Record Win: 5-0 (1888/89)
Record Defeat: 3-9 (1934/35)

HULL CITY
P50 W18 D16 L16
Record Win: 7-1 (1929/30)
Record Defeat: 1-5 (1909/10)

IPSWICH TOWN
P64 W20 D14 L30
Record Win: 6-1 (1962/63)
Record Defeat: 0-7 (1976/77)

IPSWICH TOWN

LEEDS UNITED
P74 W28 D15 L31
Record Win: 6-3 (1934/35)
Record Defeat: 1-5 (1969/70)

MIDDLESBROUGH

P88 W31 D21 L36
Record Win: 6-3 (1934/35)
Record Defeat: 0-4 (1973/74, 2004/05)

MILLWALL

P32 W10 D9 L13
Record Win: 6-1 (1929/30)
Record Defeat: 1-4 (1987/88, 1990/91)

NORWICH CITY

P52 W22 D13 L17
Record Win: 5-1 (1996/97)
Record Defeat: 0-4 (2012/13)

NOTTINGHAM FOREST

P114 W51 D23 L40
Record Win: 8-0 (1899/1900)
Record Defeat: 1-6 (1899/1900, 1900/01)

PRESTON NORTH END

P98 W37 D24 L37
Record Win: 4-0 (1959/60)
Record Defeat: 0-5 (1888/89, 1889/90, 1894/95)

PRESTON NORTH END

QPR

QPR

P38 W16 D9 L13
Record Win: 5-1 (2007/08)
Record Defeat: 1-4 (2014/15)

READING

P30 W17 D6 L7
Record Win: 5-0 (1928/29)
Record Defeat: 3-5 (1928/29)

ROTHERHAM UNITED

P6 W2 D2 L2
Record Win: 3-0 (2003/04)
Record Defeat: 1-2 (2001/02)

SHEFFIELD UNITED

P104 W39 D25 L40
Record Win: 4-0 (1922/23, 1987/88)
Record Defeat: 0-6 (1999/2000)

SHEFFIELD WEDNESDAY

P106 W31 D25 L50
Record Win: 6-0 (1894/95)
Record Defeat: 0-6 (1892/93)

STOKE CITY

P138 W43 D35 L60
Record Win: 6-0 (1988/89)
Record Defeat: 3-10 (1936/37)

SWANSEA CITY

P38 W13 D8 L17
Record Win: 6-2 (1929/30)
Record Defeat: 1-6 (1928/29)

WIGAN ATHLETIC

P16 W6 D3 L7
Record Win: 5-1 (1992/93)
Record Defeat: 2-3 (2012/13)

*Correct as of the start of the 2018/19 season

LEEDS UNITED

STOKE CITY

Cyrille Regis

As far as the Albion is concerned, the Cyrille Regis story started with the eagle eye of scout Ronnie Allen, a man who knew a thing or two about goalscoring having scored more than 200 for the club! Allen spotted Cyrille playing non-league football for Hayes and, having seen him put ball, goalkeeper and a selection of defenders into the net when going up for a cross, decided there and then that here was a new No. 9 for an Albion desperate for a successor to Jeff Astle.

Bought as one for the future in 1977, fate moved in Cyrille's direction in the summer when John Giles resigned as Albion manager and Allen took over. Injury to Tony Brown then left a spot vacant in the League Cup side against Rotherham on August 31st. Regis was ushered into the starting XI, scored twice in a 4-0 win and instantly won over the crowd. He retained his place in the side on the Saturday when Middlesbrough came to town; a tough, rugged side.

Cyrille received the ball around half-way, turned towards goal and by the time he'd gone about 30 yards, he was dragging three – or four, or five depending on which bit of the legend you prefer – defenders, all desperately holding on to him by the shirt, the shorts, anything they could. Never mind. He simply hauled them along behind him before smashing the ball into the net from 20 yards and ensuring a 2-1 win for the Throstles. A star was born and that star never diminished from that moment.

"THEY SMASHED DOWN EVERY STUPID, LAZY STEREOTYPE THAT EXISTED ABOUT BLACK FOOTBALLERS"

Regis was a regular in the Albion side ever after, simply getting better and better. He was the focal point of the side that reached the FA Cup semi-final that season, ending his first campaign, 1977/78, with 18 goals. In the summer of 1978, he set off for China with the club and, on that trip, under the management of Ron Atkinson, the "Three Degrees" were really born, Cyrille bonding with Laurie Cunningham and the relatively newly-arrived Brendon Batson.

Between them, in the year ahead, they smashed down every stupid, lazy stereotype that existed about black footballers, dazzled the nation and spearheaded a wave of black talent that ultimately became central to our national game.

Another 17 goals followed for Cyrille in that 1978/79 season that still rings down the ages and is still the benchmark by which Albion sides are judged, the blueprint to which they are asked to aspire. After a tough following season with injury, the great man was back in business in 1980/81 with 17 goals as Albion finished fourth in the First Division. Then came his best individual campaign, significantly under Ronnie Allen, back as manager.

With Bryan Robson and Remi Moses following Atkinson to Manchester United – he wanted Cyrille and Derek Statham too but didn't dare come back for them – Regis took on the responsibility of holding things together. He smashed in 25 goals, keeping Albion in the top flight, powering us towards the semi-finals of both the League Cup and FA Cup.

Finally, having scored three goals in six England Under-21 appearances and played in three B internationals too, he collected his first senior England cap after far too long a wait, coming on as a substitute against Northern Ireland at Wembley in the Home International game on February 23rd 1982. He figured as a sub against Wales at Ninian Park in April and was named in the provisional 40-man squad for the World Cup in Spain that summer. He got his first England start in Reykjavik as England took on Iceland in a warm-up game on June 2nd but came off with a hamstring injury and withdrew from the squad, a bitter blow.

He started against West Germany the following October, lasting 80 minutes before being replaced and that was essentially that, one last England cap coming against Turkey, again as a sub, in October 1987. By then, he had left The Hawthorns having, by his own admission, lost his way a little. Ruthlessly self-critical in later life, he conceded that after that World Cup disappointment, his dedication waned a little and though he remained the darling of the crowd and started to form a handy partnership with Garry Thompson, things were not as they had been.

On September 29th

1984, he played in a 2-1 defeat to Manchester United at The Hawthorns and, after a career of 297 starts and five substitute appearances, 111 goals and a million memories, Cyrille's Albion career was done.

He moved to Coventry for £250,00, something he admitted was a huge blow to his ego after being valued at £750,000 by St Etienne just six years before, but it turned out for the best in the end as he collected the FA Cup winner's medal that had eluded him with the Albion, along with that final England cap.

"THEY DON'T MAKE THEM LIKE CYRILLE REGIS ANY MORE. THEY NEVER DID..."

Shattered by the death of his friend Laurie Cunningham in a car crash in 1989, Cyrille re-evaluated his personal and professional life, got himself into as good a shape as ever and extended his career beyond Coventry, through spells at the Villa, Wolves, Wycombe Wanderers and Chester City until calling it a day in October 1996 at the age of 38.

Coaching beckoned and he was back home, back with the Albion, taking charge of the team in a caretaker capacity too before leaving shortly after the arrival of Gary Megson in 2000. From there, there was a role as an agent and a mentor, there was time as an ambassador for Christians In Sport and Water Aid and there was a well-deserved MBE in 2008, though how it wasn't a peerage, who knows.

They don't make them like Cyrille Regis any more. They never did.

THE ALBION FOUNDATION DELIVERS AGAIN!

TOGETHER WE ARE ALBION

THE ALBION FOUNDATION WAS BUSY AGAIN THROUGHOUT 2018 DELIVERING EDUCATION PACKAGES TO PUPILS ACROSS THE AREA, offering coaching courses for budding players, working in disability sports, helping Blind Dave with his "Colour Run" and promoting Equality & Diversity within our support amongst a host of other initiatives.

We had 18,008 participants in our sessions.

We engaged with 3,517 disabled people.

Of those, 9,603 went to a session for the first time.

We delivered an incredible 579,907 hours of education and sport-related work with participants.

The Foundation worked in over 200 schools.

We fielded 31 representative teams in all sporting arenas.

Makes you proud to be an Albion fan, doesn't it?!

We have 157 disabled players registered with us.

ANSWERS

WORDSEARCH (P33)

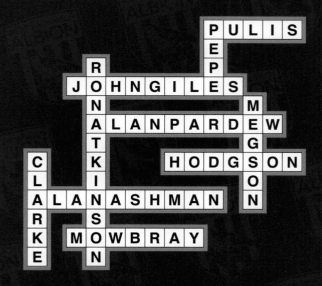

N	K	L	R	K	D	F	F	C	K	R	P	Y
L	B	H	Y	G	L	D	C	J	Z	N	N	S
V	T	R	O	B	E	R	T	S	L	E	K	P
M	X	K	T	B	J	J	Z	U	N	L	R	I
H	M	B	R	O	W	N	K	O	L	L	N	L
T	K	T	T	T	P	A	S	N	H	A	T	L
H	A	K	P	L	K	D	S	V	W	E	N	I
U	X	Y	F	U	R	T	W	I	L	B	V	H
N	D	W	L	A	H	T	R	T	G	R	Q	P
T	L	O	H	O	T	H	S	H	N	E	J	T
C	D	C	B	L	R	A	D	L	R	C	R	R
E	I	G	N	I	W	M	E	D	O	V	V	K
R	N	X	R	N	E	T	K	L	K	Y	F	G

CROSSWORD (P18)

```
                        P U L I S
                        E
              R         P
        J O H N G I L E S
        O     A         M
        A L A N P A R D E W
        T                 G
  C     K         H O D G S O N
  L     I                 S
  A L A N A S H M A N     O
  R     S                 N
  K     O
  E   M O W B R A Y
        N
```

QUIZ (P34–35)

1. Hibernian
2. Jason Roberts
3. Thomas Gaardsøe
4. Georges Santos & Patrick Suffo
5. Stephen Pearson
6. Walsall
7. Gary Megson
8. True, Albion won 2-0.
9. David Mills
10. Kim Do-Heon & Chris Brunt
11. 2007
12. The City Ground
13. Victor Anichebe
14. Salomón Rondón
15. True. All the previous 32 league games have been at Championship level.
16. Roy Hodgson
17. It finished 5-2 to Bolton
18. Wales
19. James Morrison
20. True, in 1888 and 1954, and Albion won both!
21. Shane Long
22. Cyrille Regis
23. Gareth Barry

MAZE (P51)

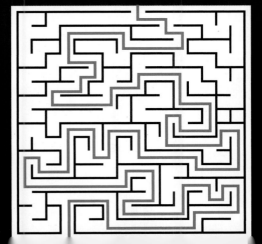

SPOT THE BALL (P45)

WEST BROMWICH ALBION
TEAM 2018/19